DISCARD

DISCARD

THE TRUTH ABOUT THE FOOD SUPPLY™

POULTRY

FROM THE FARM TO YOUR TABLE

DANIEL E. HARMON

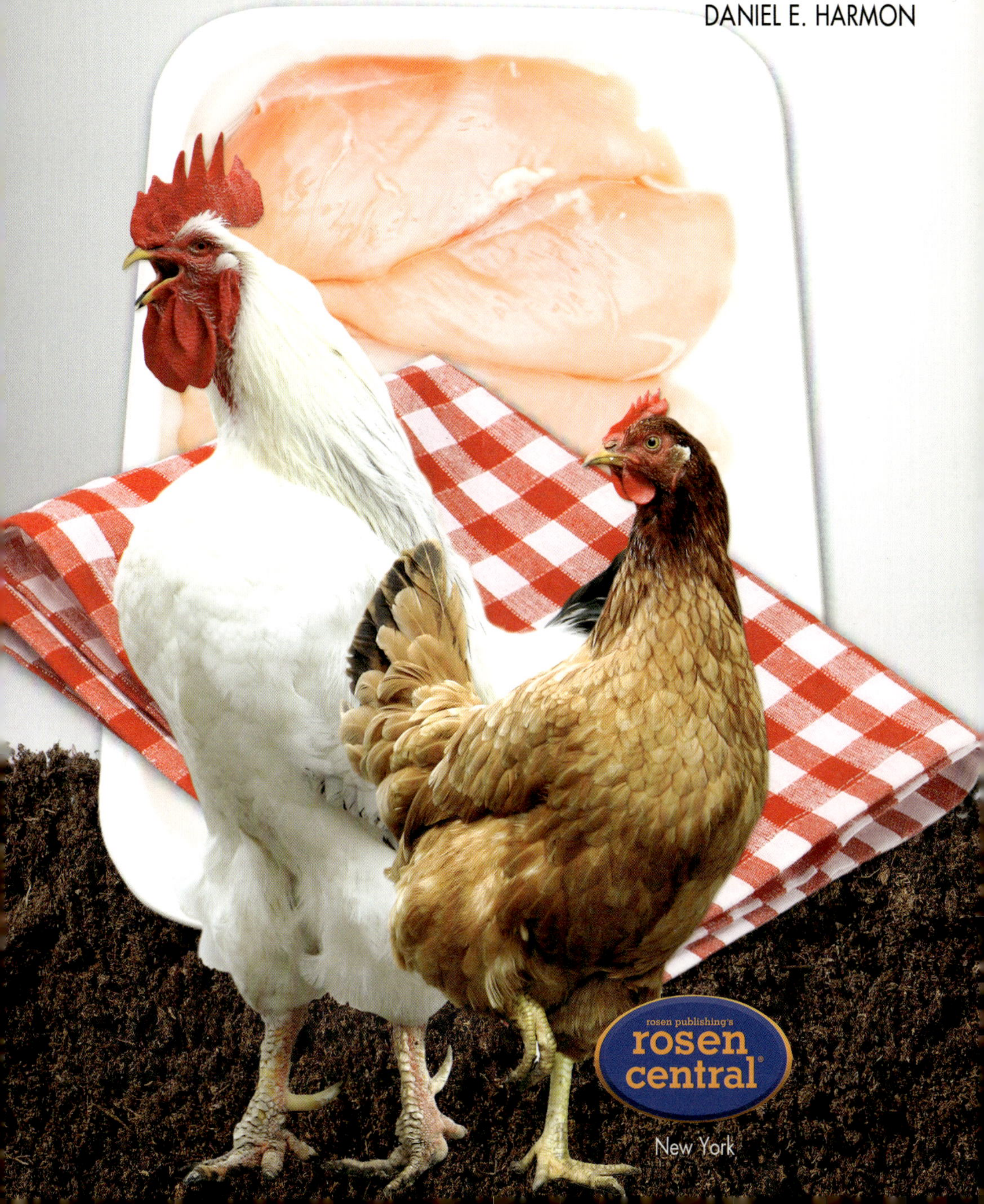

rosen publishing's
rosen central®

New York

Published in 2013 by The Rosen Publishing Group, Inc.
29 East 21st Street, New York, NY 10010

Copyright © 2013 by The Rosen Publishing Group, Inc.

First Edition

All rights reserved. No part of this book may be reproduced in any form without permission in writing from the publisher, except by a reviewer.

Library of Congress Cataloging-in-Publication Data

Harmon, Daniel E.
Poultry: from the farm to your table/Daniel E. Harmon.
    p. cm.—(The truth about the food supply)
Includes bibliographical references and index.
ISBN 978-1-4488-6798-1 (library binding)
1. Poultry—Juvenile literature. 2. Poultry industry—Juvenile literature. 3. Poultry as food—Juvenile literature. 4. Food—Safety measures. I. Title.
SF487.5.H367 2013
338.4'766493—dc23

2011039475

Manufactured in the United States of America

CPSIA Compliance Information: Batch #S12YA: For further information, contact Rosen Publishing, New York, New York, at 1-800-237-9932.

CONTENTS

INTRODUCTION
4

CHAPTER 1
WHERE DOES POULTRY COME FROM?
7

CHAPTER 2
RAISING POULTRY
15

CHAPTER 3
POULTRY PROCESSING AND PACKAGING
22

CHAPTER 4
HEALTH AND SAFETY ISSUES
29

CHAPTER 5
SMARTER, MORE SENSITIVE POULTRY FARMING AND PROCESSING
37

GLOSSARY
42

FOR MORE INFORMATION
43

FOR FURTHER READING
45

BIBLIOGRAPHY
46

INDEX
47

INTRODUCTION

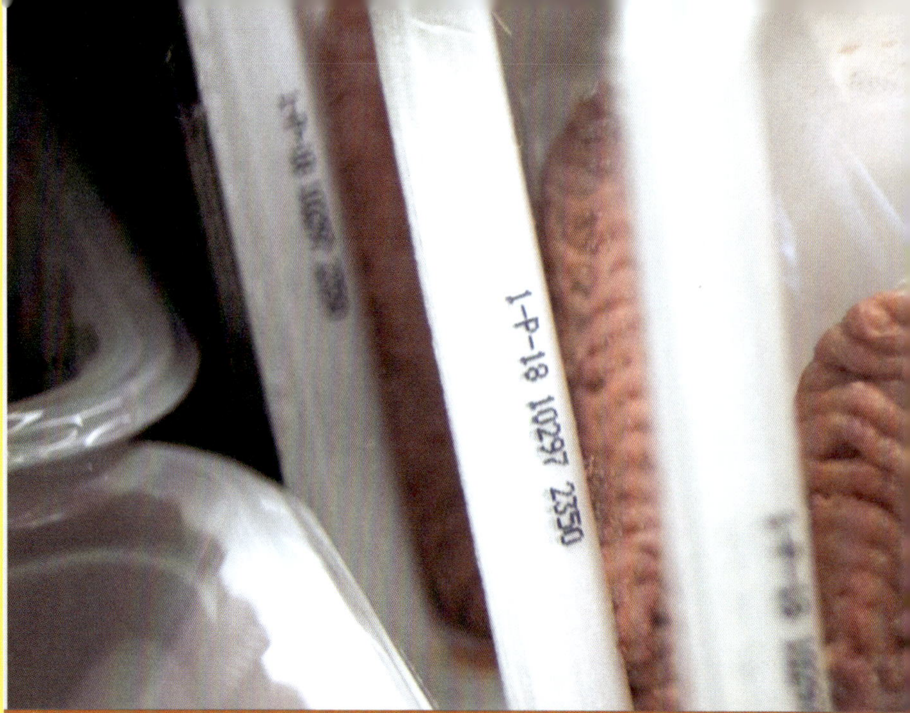

Salmonellosis is among the most widely reported food poisons. *Salmonella spp.* is a foodborne bacterium that can cause intestinal infection and other illnesses in people who accidentally eat it.

Most victims of salmonellosis poisoning recover within a week, without treatment. For some, diarrhea and other abdominal problems are so severe, they need to be hospitalized. For an elderly woman in Sacramento, California, *Salmonella* poisoning in 2011 was fatal. The culprit was believed to be ground turkey distributed by a major meat corporation.

Contamination outbreaks sometimes force the recall of packaged food products from grocery shelves. A recent example was an alarm over poisoned ground turkey meat.

Her death was part of an unfolding tragedy that began in a different part of the United States. Over a period of months, the Centers for Disease Control and Prevention (CDC) identified more than one hundred illnesses that may have been related. The victims were between the ages of one and eighty-nine. They lived in regions from the Canadian border to the West Coast to the Gulf Coast.

Several supermarket chains were among the sellers of the suspected turkey. The corporation that distributed it recalled 36 million pounds (16.4 million kilograms) of meat by September.

The 2011 salmonellosis tragedy was the latest in a string of food poisonings in contaminated poultry products. In late 2000, the bacterium *Listeria monocytogenes* was detected in turkey products sold in supermarkets and restaurants. The distributor recalled more than 16 million pounds (7.3 million kg) of meat that possibly was contaminated. Four consumer deaths were blamed on the outbreak. Also suspected were several deaths of unborn children whose pregnant mothers were poisoned.

The possibility of poisoning by salmonellosis or listeriosis is remote. It is a complication, though, in producing one of the nation's favorite foods: poultry. Americans spend $40 billion every year on chicken products alone, according to the National Chicken Council. The average American eats more than 80 pounds (36 kg) of chicken each year. Poultry providers must take great care to avoid poisoning crises.

Many people who enjoy chicken, turkey, and other types of poultry never think about how the meat gets from the farm to their table. If they investigated, it's possible poultry would not be quite so popular. It's been said that if you love hot dogs, you don't want to see them being made. The same is true of poultry products, from chicken nuggets to spicy wings to Thanksgiving turkeys.

Almost all the food people buy in supermarkets and restaurants is processed carefully and is safe to eat (although it may be fatty and otherwise unhealthy). Poultry unquestionably has nutritional value. Critics of America's food industry, however, voice concern about how some of the food is produced and processed. At times, flaws in the system result in disaster.

This book will look at how poultry is grown, processed, and marketed, from hatchling to tabletop fare.

CHAPTER 1

WHERE DOES POULTRY COME FROM?

European settlers began bringing chickens and livestock to America five hundred years ago. From then until the 1800s, most poultry was raised by families for their own consumption and for trading.

Food packaging and refrigerated transportation advanced in the late 1800s. This meant poultry and other raw food products could be distributed outside local markets. Small commercial poultry farms began to supply distant consumers.

Since World War II (1939–1945), poultry has become more popular than ever. Besides chicken dishes prepared at home, people love poultry-based fast food and

Chicken nuggets and wings, among the most popular fast-food items today, have led to skyrocketing poultry demands.

POULTRY
FROM THE FARM TO YOUR TABLE

preprepared, frozen dinners—convenient, cheap meals. Today, they especially love chicken nuggets and wings. The National Chicken Council estimated almost fourteen billion wings would be sold in 2011, mostly at restaurants.

A poultry "industry" rose to meet the demand. By the early 1960s, food corporations had established vast chicken lots and egg farms. The number of privately controlled poultry farms began to shrink, while the size of the average farming operation increased.

Egg production likewise advanced. As early as 1889, farmers and researchers were experimenting with artificial lighting in chicken coops to stimulate egg laying. A typical farm hen in the late nineteenth century laid approximately one hundred eggs in a year. By the late twentieth century, the average yearly production was more than 250 eggs.

Poultry's Rise in Popularity

Beef was the meat of choice in America until 1992. Statistics for that year indicated Americans were eating more chicken than beef. A major reason for the popularity of chicken was the phenomen of chicken nuggets.

But chickens and turkeys have always been among America's favorite foods. Part of the reason is that they are relatively easy to produce and inexpensive to buy.

The National Chicken Council reports that in the United States, more than 90 percent of the chickens sold for human consumption are produced by "independent farmers working

WHERE DOES POULTRY COME FROM?

under contract with integrated [combined] chicken production and processing companies." Individual growers produce less than 1 percent. The rest are grown on company farms.

Chicken Breeds and Types

Hundreds of chicken breeds exist around the world. About sixty are common in the United States.

All hens lay eggs, and their meat can be eaten. Different breeds are most useful for either meat or egg production. The poultry industry focuses on two general types of chickens. Broilers are fattened quickly and sold for their meat value. Layers produce eggs. "Dual-purpose" birds produce eggs and in time are slaughtered for their meat.

Most chickens and turkeys are produced industrially, raised in close quarters and processed en masse.

POULTRY
FROM THE FARM TO YOUR TABLE

A hybrid of the Cornish breed is the most common broiler raised in the United States. Seven weeks is the average life span of a broiler.

Many different breeds are raised as layers. Laying hens live much longer than broilers. Layers don't begin producing eggs until nineteen weeks. They are active egg layers for about a year.

Chicken fanciers and chefs say "heritage" (historic) chicken breeds are healthier and taste better than the newer "engineered" breeds in mass production. Historic breeds have reproduced for centuries. More than three dozen of these original breeds are now endangered.

Heritage poultry is notably leaner because it is a "working" bird. That is, it moves around, constantly searching for food. It has a much smaller breast than industry-produced chickens. Its meat takes longer to cook.

Turkeys and Other Poultry Species

Chickens are the most popular American food in the poultry category. Many consumers, however, prefer turkey meat. Turkeys are in especially great demand for Thanksgiving and Christmas feasts.

The American Poultry Association recognizes eight domesticated turkey breeds. Approximately 99 percent of turkey meat consumed in America is from the Broad-Breasted White.

Americans eat less-common types of poultry in addition to chicken and turkey. Some are game birds. Fine restaurants often

WHERE DOES POULTRY COME FROM?

include duck and goose items on their menus. More unusual are pheasant, quail, partridge, guinea, pigeon, peafowl, and ostrich. At home, many cooks prepare small Cornish game hens for special occasions.

Eggs

People around the world have eaten eggs for many centuries. Eggs are not just a breakfast food. Cooked alone or combined with various menu items, they are served at every meal and at special feasts. Eggs are popular not merely because people like them, but because they are nutritious.

Hen eggs are the most common eaten by Americans. On the average, a hen lays 259 eggs a year. People also eat the eggs of other poultry species, particularly in gourmet restaurants and at festive meals prepared at home. Edible eggs include those of turkeys, bantams, ducks, and guinea fowl. Menus even include small quail eggs and giant ostrich eggs. An omelet made with an ostrich egg can serve as many as ten diners.

Chicken eggs are graded by size from small to jumbo and packaged in cartons.

POULTRY
FROM THE FARM TO YOUR TABLE

What's in That Chicken Nugget You're Eating?

Chicken nuggets were invented in 1983. Because chickens have no "nugget" body parts, you might ask what, exactly, a chicken nugget is.

It's a manufactured product. Michael Pollan, author of *The Omnivore's Dilemma* and other works on food production and processing, has identified thirty-eight ingredients contained in a popular brand of chicken nugget. Chicken is the primary ingredient, of course. A third of the additional ingredients are corn-based. Nuggets also contain chemicals. Chemicals prevent foaming while the nuggets are being fried, prevent the fat from spoiling, and preserve freshness in the box.

Pollan objects to the corn content, which he believes is unhealthy. Chicken nuggets, he writes in *The Omnivore's Dilemma*, "are really corn wrapped up in more corn. The chicken was fed corn. The batter is made from corn flour. The starch that holds it together is cornstarch. The oil it was fried in was corn oil."

He observes that six chicken nuggets sold by that particular food provider have almost twice the fat of a typical hamburger.

WHERE DOES POULTRY COME FROM?

The National Turkey Federation points out that most turkey eggs are used to produce more turkeys. Turkey eggs sold for food taste much like chicken eggs but are more expensive.

Chicken eggs go to market graded. They are sorted by weight: small, medium, large, extra large, and jumbo. (Turkey eggs are not graded.) Most are sold to household consumers in grocery stores and farmers' markets. Food processing companies also buy eggs directly from producers to use as ingredients in countless grocery items.

Poultry Farming: A Changing Way of Life

The way the food industry has changed in the last half century

Chickens in a large barn are raised in identical lots, all born on the same day and slaughtered together.

has led to a dangerous situation, critics believe. Mark Winne, author of *Food Rebels, Guerrilla Gardeners, and Smart-Cookin' Mamas*, worries that "the industrial food system has become a tsunami that might very well engulf everything in its path." Food activists say it is unwise to drive small farmers out of business or turn them into "food factories" controlled by a handful of giant corporations.

In many situations, it costs factory farmers more to raise poultry than they will be paid for their efforts. For example, it may cost a farmer $300,000 to build a chicken house. The farmer must go into debt to build it—and may never earn enough to pay off the debt.

Farming has always been risky. Anything that goes wrong can cost farmers a lot of money. In some circumstances, one mishap can put them out of business.

Extended hundred-degree temperatures in July 2011 led to tens of thousands of poultry deaths in North Carolina and Kansas. A power outage briefly turned off cooling systems at one farm, resulting in ten thousand chickens perishing. At a turkey farm, it took workers a day and night to bury more than 4,300 dead birds.

CHAPTER 2

Raising Poultry

Seven weeks. That's the life span of most broiler chickens raised in the United States. Seven weeks after they hatch, they're slaughtered and their meat is processed for sale to consumers. They have become as plump as they're going to get. To keep them alive longer would cost poultry growers additional money for feed and housing.

Poultry "Factories"

Most of the chickens people consume are raised and processed in almost exactly the same way. They live their lives packed by the thousand in fenced yards or large barns called grow-out houses. Producers feed them basically the same processed food, and they live the same number of days. Farms are operated largely with machines. The poultry industry determines what kinds of equipment growers must use.

The routine is similar in turkey production. In effect, most commercial poultry is mass-produced and processed. So are most other foods, including beef, vegetables, and fruit. In a way, it is the

POULTRY
FROM THE FARM TO YOUR TABLE

same basic industrial system that produces cars, computers, and other goods.

Around 1900, turkey farmers began selling their birds according to weight. To receive top dollar, they learned they could pump up the bird's weight for market. They stuffed it with food during the weeks before it was slaughtered. In some cases, they force-fed their turkeys.

The average weight of a six-month-old tom (male) turkey in 1920 was 21.6 pounds (9.8 kg). By the end of the century, toms

Animal rights groups decry the cramped caging of chickens at factory farms. Even when not caged, the birds spend practically all their lives in close confinement.

RAISING POULTRY

were being sent to market two months younger—and 5 pounds (2.3 kg) heavier.

As with chicken farming, the trend in recent decades has been to raise fewer turkeys on the open range, more in confinement. Rarer poultry types such as ducks and quail also are raised commercially in fast-growth, low-cost conditions.

The popularity of fast food in the mid-1900s gave rise to today's industrial food production system. You may avoid fast food. Still, the meat you eat at home is probably produced under the same conditions as that produced for fast-food restaurants.

Food companies have practical objectives. They need to produce as much food for market as possible, quickly. They must use the smallest area of farmland

WHAT ARE CAFOs?

A few giant corporations control much of the poultry, livestock, grain, and vegetable farming in the United States today. At a supermarket, you see countless food brands. If you look closely at the labels, however, you may find that the brand is owned by one of a handful of large companies. These corporate owners control how most poultry and other food types are produced.

Corporations contract with farmers to produce the raw products. By and large, poultry are raised in what are known as CAFOs: "confined/concentrated animal feeding operations." David Kirby, author of *Animal Factory*, describes them as "large-scale, mechanized megafarms where hundreds of thousands of cows, pigs, chickens, and turkeys are fed and fattened for market, all within the confines of enclosed buildings or crowded outdoor lots."

possible. To keep store prices low, they must keep their production costs low.

Growers have found that they can keep costs down by using a formula for production. If all their chickens and turkeys are raised under identical conditions, it simplifies processing. That means lower costs. Raising poultry animals in severe confinement saves even more.

The Ideal Bird

Agricultural scientists have learned farmers can produce more food faster by controlling its very makeup, or genetics. This is called genetic engineering. They can raise chickens "intensively," thousands to a shed, each bird looking and weighing exactly the same. Each bird is born on the same day and reaches maturity on the same day. "Maturity" means the chicken is fat enough to be slaughtered and processed.

Chickens produced on industrial farms today are unlike those farmers raised a century ago. As noted in the last chapter, they neither look nor taste quite the same. They have been "redesigned" through breeding experiments.

One result of modern farming techniques is that chickens have larger breasts. Food companies grow them that way on purpose. Studies show that people prefer white meat.

Eric Schlosser and Charles Wilson, in their book *Chew On This*, report that an industrially raised young chicken puts on some 5.5 pounds (2.5 kg) in a little more than a month. "If a child

RAISING POULTRY

A farmer feeds a flock of free-range chickens. At many free-range farms, the chickens spend very little time outdoors roaming the farmyard.

gained weight that fast, he or she would weigh 286 pounds [130 kg] by the age of six."

Fattiness and other growing conditions cause many chickens to die before they're ready for slaughter. Mass-produced chickens live their whole lives in artificial lighting and never go outside. They are fed processed food designed to fatten them quickly. In the old days, chickens foraged over the ground and grass for insects and seeds. Modern chicken feed contains mainly corn and other grains.

POULTRY
FROM THE FARM TO YOUR TABLE

Some poultry feed additives are beneficial. An example is flaxseed. Farmers in recent years have fed it to laying hens to increase health-friendly omega-3 fatty acids.

Free-Range Poultry

Much has been written about "free-range" poultry. In theory, free-range chickens are grown the old-fashioned way. They eat things chickens naturally eat: worms, insects, fly larvae, and other morsels they peck from the ground and from unfertilized, untreated grass. They have the run of the farm. They spend much of their time in the sunshine and fresh air. As a result of their organic upbringing, they are healthier than chickens that spend their lives in tight confinement being fed processed feed. They provide healthier meals for humans.

Some free-range birds actually live that way, basically. At other organic farms, there's a striking similarity between the production of free-range and confined chickens. Michael Pollan, in his book *The Omnivore's Dilemma*, described what he saw at one free-range chicken farm.

Some twenty thousand chickens occupy a large shed. A small door opens to a narrow strip of yard. However, the chickens aren't allowed outside until they are five weeks old—just two weeks before slaughter. "By that time," Pollan writes, "they are so used to the shed that none of them go outside."

The U.S. Department of Agriculture (USDA) requires that chickens labeled "free-range" have access to the open air. Regulations

RAISING POULTRY

do not define the open area. It can be hard-packed dirt, not grass. There is no minimum required time that they must spend outside.

Some chickens on the market are considered "organic" in the sense that their food does not contain additives. Additives include antibiotics to prevent infections.

Interestingly, the lack of antibiotics makes these chickens especially susceptible to diseases. Pollan notes that "if one gets sick, they will all get sick. An infection could kill 20,000 birds overnight." That's why they are raised under conditions in which they are not encouraged to "go outside and catch a cold."

Truly organic poultry raised on grassland is desirable. Pollan explains, "When cattle, chickens, and other animals eat grass—and not just corn or other grains—they are actually healthier for us to eat. So is the milk and eggs that come from grass-fed animals."

Here, chickens on a Nebraska farm actually forage for food in the open grass, benefiting from a healthier natural diet.

CHAPTER 3
POULTRY PROCESSING AND PACKAGING

Some of the labels and advertisements for poultry items portray sunny, peaceful farm scenes. In reality, most chicken and turkey farms are not pleasant places to visit. The chickens don't wander happily around barnyards and fields. You'll find them stuffed inside sheds, twenty-four hours a day.

The farms are not as gross, though, as the slaughterhouses. Before it gets to your table, that bird from "Happy Acres" undergoes a series of grim, violent processes.

END OF A LIFE, BEGINNING OF A MEAL

Eric Schlosser and Charles Wilson, in their book *Chew On This*, describe how chickens meet their deaths. Most commercially produced chickens "are killed at enormous slaughterhouses, hanging upside down, their legs shackled to a fast-moving chain that carries thousands of birds . . . [O]ne animal after another is killed and then rapidly taken apart."

POULTRY PROCESSING AND PACKAGING

Most chickens are processed in assembly-line fashion, as shown at this North Carolina facility. While human workers are required for essential tasks, much of the processing is done by machines.

Schlosser and Wilson go into gruesome details about how the birds die. In some slaughterhouses in Europe, chickens are gassed to death in chambers. Compared to other methods of slaughter, gassing is a less painful way for a chicken to go.

At major slaughterhouses in the United States, live turkeys and chickens are slaughtered mechanically. The equipment dips their heads into electrified water to stun them. An automated blade cuts their throats. Dousing the corpses in scalding water loosens the feathers for easy plucking. All of this, at large slaughterhouses, can be done with machines.

Laborers then sever the heads, remove the insides, and dress the de-feathered birds for shipment. Carcasses are either cut into pieces (breasts, drumsticks, etc.) or kept whole.

In small slaughterhouses, some procedures, such as cutting the throats, are done by hand.

Poultry parts are chilled immediately. Then they are packed, frozen, and sent to market. The U.S. Department of Agriculture's Food Safety and Inspection Service (FSIS) is authorized to prevent processing plants from using inferior wraps and containers. It requires plant owners to obtain written statements from packaging providers, guaranteeing that the products comply with food regulations.

Workers in poultry processing plants must obey careful standards of hygiene. Food handlers can spread bacterial diseases that affect the meat products.

Additives

When food companies process raw meats or plants for human consumption, they usually apply artificial additives. Additives are intended for your good. Skeptics, though, question whether all additives are necessary. Some additives, industry critics say, can actually hurt you.

In poultry processing, additives are applied as early as the scalding step. Their purpose at that stage is to kill salmonellosis and any other potential poisons immediately.

POULTRY PROCESSING AND PACKAGING

Using the Entire Bird

Breasts, thighs, drumsticks, and wings are the parts of poultry usually placed before you on the dinner table. Processors find other uses for less valuable meat. Even nonedible poultry parts can be sold for various purposes.

Mature layers that have stopped laying eggs or become physically damaged are called "spent hens." Although not prime meat, they can be processed and used. They provide ingredients for chicken soup and salad. They are also processed in hot dogs, baloney, and other food products that contain blended ingredients. Turkey meat, too, may be found in food items that might seem strange, such as sausage, bacon, and pepperoni.

After slaughter, chicken entrails, feathers, and blood can be used to make compost. Compost is a naturally produced fertilizer. Like artificial fertilizers, it is spread across crop fields to enrich the soil.

Chicken remains are also used in making feed for cattle, swine, and poultry. They are used to manufacture products such as bird bedding. Feathers are used in making decorative items.

POULTRY
FROM THE FARM TO YOUR TABLE

Government regulations require food companies to reveal on labels what a product contains.

The FSIS observes that food additives have been used for thousands of years. "Additives are used for flavor and appeal, food preparation and processing, freshness, and safety." The FSIS and the U.S. Food and Drug Administration (FDA) are responsible for ensuring the safety of additives.

Additives include coloring chemicals. Dyes are used to highlight the visual appeal of foods. That's OK, regulations say, as long as coloring chemicals aren't used to cover up dangerous flaws or to otherwise fool buyers. Government rules require that food labels indicate whether dyes are among the ingredients. Additives may also include flavorings.

Consumer activists long have questioned the use of additives. Additives came under close examination after certain food dyes were linked to cancer.

PROCESSING EGGS

In addition to grading eggs (small to jumbo), egg processors check them for damage before sending them to market. One process they use for this is called candling.

26

POULTRY PROCESSING AND PACKAGING

An expert candler at a Montana processing plant scrutinizes eggs passing over a light table, looking for flaws. Candling helps suppliers sort out bad eggs before they reach the supermarket.

In candling, light-sensitive equipment scans eggs. It automatically finds cracked shells. Remarkably, it can see defects inside an egg. As eggs pass over a conveyor belt, candling technology culls the bad ones.

Federal law regulates how eggs must be transported from processing plants to supermarkets. For example, eggs in transit must be kept at temperatures below 41 degrees Fahrenheit (4.5 degrees Celsius).

POULTRY
FROM THE FARM TO YOUR TABLE

MYTHS AND FACTS

Myth: Industrially grown chickens and turkeys are given steroids to increase their size.
Fact: Steroids and other growth hormones are used to produce larger cows, but they are prohibited for poultry. Some poultry meat and egg producers have advertised that their products are hormone-free. Critics point out that the claim is meaningless because it holds true for rival poultry products, too.

Myth: Roosters are involved in the egg production process.
Fact: Laying hens don't require roosters to help them produce the eggs that humans eat. Roosters must be involved to produce eggs that will hatch into chicks.

Myth: Eggs are an especially safe food because of their protective shells.
Fact: Chickens contaminated with salmonellosis and other poisons can pass those dangers along in the eggs they lay. Even fresh eggs can be contaminated, which is why workers must sanitize them immediately after they are laid. Eggs may have hairline cracks that admit bacteria. Although they feel hard, eggshells are very thin and fragile. If stored near smelly foods, eggs can absorb the aroma and flavor. Dieticians recommend that eggs not be kept in the refrigerator longer than two weeks.

CHAPTER 4
Health and Safety Issues

Until recent years, dieticians considered poultry meat and eggs vital for good health. Chicken and turkey meat provides a rich source of protein. At the same time, it is low in fat, compared to red meat.

Hen eggs are rich in protein, calcium, zinc, iron, riboflavin, thiamin, and vitamins A, B12, D, E, and K. They contribute to a healthy immune system and strong bones and joints. Turkey eggs, roughly 50 percent larger than hen eggs, are especially rich in vitamin E—but contain more fat and cholesterol. (Turkey *meat*, on the other hand, is lower in fat content than other meats.)

Some nutritionists today, notably vegan advocates, insist that humans can live well without poultry products. They point out that other foods provide those nutrients.

Besides nutritional values, industry watchers are interested in other health-related issues.

Production and Processing Concerns

Food scientists believe poultry grown in tight, strictly controlled confinement is less healthy to eat than free-roaming poultry.

POULTRY
FROM THE FARM TO YOUR TABLE

Studies have indicated fat levels are higher in chickens that are mass-produced.

Part of the reason is the food that's fed to confined chickens. Author Michael Pollan, in his book *In Defense of Food*, takes the "you are what you eat" slogan a step further: "You are what what you eat eats too." That is, the quality of the meat you eat is affected by the quality of the food those animals ate when they were alive. Pollan writes: "Even animals that do well on grain, such as chickens and pigs, are much healthier when they have access to green plants, and so, it turns out, are their meat and eggs."

An egg farmer sprays a chemical to kill flies in the waste beneath his chicken cages. Insects can transmit flu and other diseases dangerous in poultry production.

HEALTH AND SAFETY ISSUES

Besides grain, some chicken feed contains disgusting ingredients. In *Chew On This*, authors Eric Schlosser and Charles Wilson state, "Chicken feed is often made out of whatever can be bought inexpensively." That may include waste from cattle and poultry slaughterhouses. "The aim is to provide feed that will fatten chickens as quickly and as cheaply as possible."

Sanitation in poultry houses has been a highly publicized concern. Bird droppings are ever present. Dust and feathers fly. Germs pose hazards to the birds and the humans who work there.

Industry watchers worry that packaged meat and eggs can be contaminated if they aren't processed properly. They also worry about some of the things added intentionally during processing. Regulations permit food coloring and flavor enhancers. Some of those substances, though, may cause unhealthy reactions in people who regularly eat the products. The dye tartrazine, for example, is suspected of causing skin rashes and headaches and may contribute to childhood asthma. Carmine, another dye, has triggered serious allergies.

Some whole and cut poultry meat undergoes irradiation during processing. Irradiation destroys germs and prevents foodborne illness. Critics say it also poses health hazards because it produces radioactive waste.

FOOD CONTAMINATION

Listeria monocytogenes, a bacterium potentially fatal to humans, can infect poultry and meat if processing safety is ignored. It

POULTRY
FROM THE FARM TO YOUR TABLE

The circular inset image shows the microscopic *Salmonella spp.* bacteria that can infect raw chicken and turkey meat.

can also invade the by-products, eggs, and milk. The disease can further weaken people who suffer from cancer and other illnesses. It can cause pregnant women to miscarry and can injure unborn children.

Shigella spp. is another bacterium that has infected poultry, as well as vegetables and dairy products. A slight amount of it can lead to abdominal disorders. It can cause serious diseases like Reiter's syndrome, which results in swollen joints and inflamed eyes.

Campylobacter jejuni is sometimes found in improperly cooked chicken and other meat and in untreated milk and water. Discomforts usually are minor—fever, headache, nausea, abdominal pain, or diarrhea. In a few cases, however, it is believed to have led to more serious nerve and muscle ailments.

In the opening years of this century, the CDC noted high incidence rates of *Salmonella spp.* in raw turkeys. At least 13 percent of raw turkeys in the United States reportedly carried the dangerous bacteria. Thorough cooking kills it, but improper processing and preparation can present health threats.

HEALTH AND SAFETY ISSUES

The problem of foodborne bacteria and other poisons is complicated. Attempts to solve those problems sometimes create problems of their own. For example, a class of antibiotics called quinolones in the mid-1990s was introduced to cure chickens of certain infections. It was effective, but some strains of bacteria learned to resist quinolones. These strains presented new threats—to humans.

Proper cooking is essential to kill *Salmonella spp.* and other poisons. Cooking time is as important as cooking temperature.

Dieticians urge precautions when cooking poultry. *Campylobacter jejuni* and other causes of dietary ailments are not threats if the meat is cooked properly. Dieticians also warn against eating raw eggs. Even lightly cooked eggs should be avoided by people in fragile health and pregnant women. Food experts note that cooking temperatures and cooking times are both important.

GOVERNMENT REGULATION

Federal, state, and local government agencies became involved in ensuring food safety during the late 1800s. Today, the USDA

POULTRY
FROM THE FARM TO YOUR TABLE

DANGEROUS JOBS

In their book *Chew On This*, authors Eric Schlosser and Charles Wilson describe meatpacking as "one of the most dangerous jobs." Sharp cutting machines are standard tools of the work.

The joint Safety and Health Committee of the National Chicken Council and the National Turkey Federation has published equipment checklists. The purpose is to "help poultry companies address critical safety issues" involving new and existing equipment. The checklist covers such points as equipment design, training, ventilation, personal protective equipment, and fall protection.

is the major entity that oversees meat and poultry.

The USDA began grading eggs in 1918 and inspecting them for quality in 1928. In 1934, the department published standards for egg production. The U.S. Congress in 1957 passed the Poultry Products Inspection Act.

Another key agency is the FDA. Although not responsible for monitoring meat and poultry, the FDA inspects all other food types, including the ingredients contained in poultry feed.

In addition to passing and enforcing food regulations, the government monitors the food industry. Other organizations besides the USDA are involved. FoodNet is a network of federal and state government agencies. It checks food samples to make sure they are uncontaminated. The Canadian government has formed the Canadian Food Inspection Agency.

HEALTH AND SAFETY ISSUES

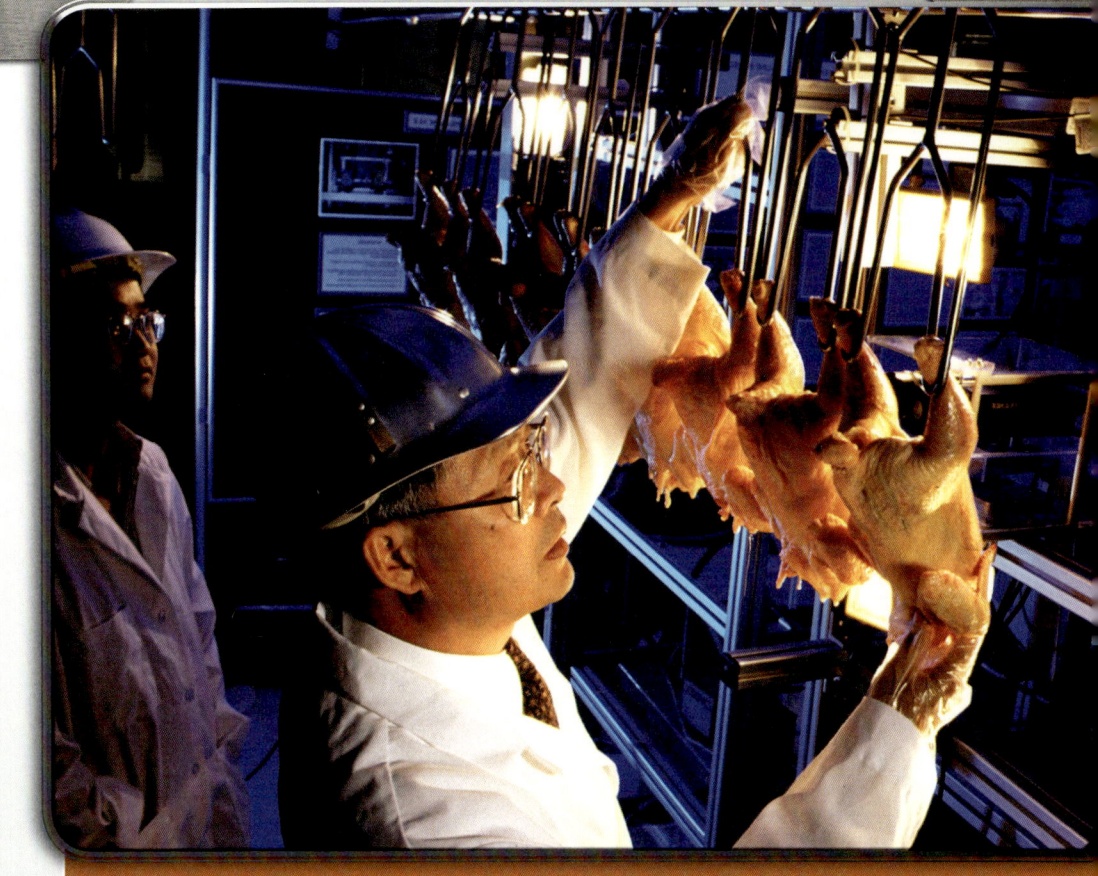

Regulatory agencies try to ensure safety in the food industry but are often understaffed. Here, a government official uses a computerized system to inspect poultry in a processing line.

The USDA and other regulatory agencies face challenges. One problem is understaffing. There aren't enough inspectors to monitor everything that goes on in poultry production. Another difficulty is that scientific testing takes time. In many cases, government watchdog agencies learn about a food hazard only when the public does—after sickness or death has occurred.

Still, the likelihood of being poisoned by bad poultry is slight.

POULTRY
FROM THE FARM TO YOUR TABLE

10 GREAT QUESTIONS TO ASK A NUTRITIONIST

1. Which is healthier: white meat or dark?
2. Is baked chicken healthier for you than fried chicken?
3. Is turkey meat better for you than chicken meat? What about the comparative nutritional values of duck, quail, and other types of poultry?
4. Are those "wings" served at restaurants good for me or bad?
5. A friend has invited us to a dinner featuring wild turkey from his recent hunting trip. Is that safe to eat? Is it more or less healthy than commercially grown turkey?
6. What's the difference between "free-range" and "cage-free" poultry?
7. Should I stop eating eggs if I have cholesterol concerns?
8. Did *Listeria monocytogenes* and other forms of poultry contamination exist a hundred years ago? Has anything changed?
9. How long can eggs and poultry meat be refrigerated or frozen before they become unsafe to eat?
10. I get drowsy after Thanksgiving dinner. Is it simply because I overeat, or is it caused by something in the turkey meat?

Chapter 5

Smarter, More Sensitive Poultry Farming and Processing

Most food industry analysts recognize the importance of poultry to the world food supply. Many believe there are better ways to produce it, though. Scientists, farmers, government agencies, and consumer watchdog organizations continue to study processes that could be improved.

Human health and safety are just two of the concerns. Another is the environment. Meanwhile, animal rights groups accuse producers of cruelty in chicken house and slaughterhouse methods. And some economists believe a return to small, local farms and markets would be good for the overall economy.

Environmental Issues

Environmentalists generally encourage consumers to buy organic foods. Besides the apparent health benefits, small, organic farming operations do not damage or wear out the land as badly as

POULTRY
FROM THE FARM TO YOUR TABLE

chemical-intensive industrial farms. In fact, some organic poultry farmers point out that by using slaughterhouse remains and waste wisely, they restore their land each year with natural fertilization.

A farmer unloads chickens at a local farmers' market. The locavore movement has become popular as more consumers have come to favor fresh, rather than processed, foods.

Cruelty Concerns

Critics of poultry production are disgusted by the animals' living conditions. In industrial chicken houses, the birds literally spend their lives squeezed together in "standing room only" confinement. They are fattened without exercise. By the time they're ready for slaughter, their legs are practically useless. Even if they were turned outside to graze, they wouldn't be able to walk.

Adult turkeys tend to be aggressive. For that reason, farmers remove the beaks and toes of young turkeys.

Pressured by animal rights activists, some poultry producers have made improvements. Around the turn of the century, a group called People for the Ethical Treatment of Animals (PETA) threatened to organize widespread protests against a major fast-food company. The reason was the appalling conditions at chicken farms that supply the company's chain restaurants. The corporation instructed

SMARTER, MORE SENSITIVE POULTRY FARMING AND PROCESSING

its suppliers to provide a few more square inches of space for laying hens. It also called on its meat suppliers to use slaughterhouse methods that caused less suffering to cattle, hogs, and chickens.

Michael Pollan, in *The Omnivore's Dilemma*, asserts, "There is no excuse for the cruelty that goes on in our factory farms and feedlots."

The "excuse," others point out, is economics—and, in the minds of many, a looming worldwide food crisis. Consumers are troubled. While their personal and family incomes remain flat, the costs of food and other necessities rise relentlessly. Many families would prefer to buy only organic products, but they must buy the cheapest food they can find. The cheapest food generally is the food that costs the least to produce.

Meanwhile, global hunger is a continuing tragic situation. Mass production, industry supporters maintain, is the only hope for meeting mass demands.

New Farming Economics: The Locavore Movement

Poultry farmers are caught in a no-win situation, say critics of giant food corporations. To compete in the market, they now must operate under contract for large meatpacking companies. Contracts favor the corporations.

Basically, the company delivers a shipment of hatchlings to a farmer. The company owns the chickens from birth to death. The farmer is hired to raise them until they are adults, ready for slaughter. The company provides chicken feed and support

READ THE LABELS

Advocates of improvements in food production and processing want to see stronger regulations and more thorough inspections. Meanwhile, individuals can become involved simply by taking greater care in their purchasing decisions. A key to wise shopping is to study food labels.

By law, food suppliers must specify the contents of food products on every label. Smart shoppers read the labels. They also research the restaurants they frequent. They find out where the food was produced and processed, exactly what it contains, and the nutritional value.

Michael Pollan in *In Defense of Food* offers a tip for buyers who want free-range poultry. To make sure the bird actually roamed grassy areas when it was alive, "look for the word 'pastured'" in the labeling.

professionals such as veterinarians. The farmer must provide the housing and equipment. The company determines what equipment the farmer must use.

Many farmers now embrace the locavore movement. Locavores are consumers who buy locally grown products. Thousands in some areas regularly show up at weekly farmers' markets. They don't mind the inconvenience of driving farther and perhaps paying more to obtain fresh products. The number of farmers' markets doubled in the late 1990s and early 2000s. Small farms increased by 20 percent between 2002 and 2008.

When customers buy directly from farmers, the farmers get most or all of the money. The way the corporate food industry works, most of the money people spend on food goes to middlemen. These include packagers,

SMARTER, MORE SENSITIVE POULTRY FARMING AND PROCESSING

everyone involved in distribution networks, and supermarket owners.

Making Choices

Industry observers expect poultry to continue to be a vital part of the human diet. Poultry is safe to eat as long as it is produced, packaged, prepared, and served according to modern health standards. Its nutritional value is proven.

Increasingly, wise young people are concerned about where their food comes from and how it gets to their tables. They Google the companies whose products they and their families frequently buy. They learn about those companies' processes and policies. They ask questions: How is their food grown? How is it processed? How should it be cooked? What are possible dangers?

By their choices, teenagers can affect poultry production. They can get to know local farmers and become involved in the locavore movement. They might try raising backyard chickens and urban gardening. Individuals of all ages can do their small part to shape a better food industry.

Young people can help promote a better food system by learning what's in their food and making wise eating choices.

GLOSSARY

additive A food color, flavor, vitamin, or other ingredient added to the base product.

antibiotic Chemical substance used mainly to kill harmful germs.

bacterium A single-cell organism that could be either harmful or beneficial to humans.

chicken fancier A person who breeds poultry to improve its quality.

comply To meet specified standards or act according to rules.

domesticate To tame an animal and keep it as a pet or for farm produce.

entrails The stomach, heart, and other waste parts of animals.

forage To search widely for food.

genetic engineering Changing an organism's DNA to create improved offspring.

genetics The study of hereditary traits of organisms.

heritage chickens Breeds that were raised many years ago.

hybrid A cross of two breeds.

incidence The frequency with which something, such as a disease, appears in a certain population or area.

irradiation Using small doses of radiation to kill germs during food processing.

organic Food grown without artificial fertilizers or pesticides, using no fossil fuel.

recall When a manufacturer requests that all the purchasers of a certain product return it, as the result of the discovery of a fault or problem.

vegan A strict vegetarian who eats no foods derived from animals.

FOR MORE INFORMATION

Canadian Food Inspection Agency (CFIA)
1400 Merivale Road
Ottawa, ON K1A 0Y9
Canada
(613) 225-2342
Web site: http://www.inspection.gc.ca
The CFIA, which is dedicated to safeguarding food, animals, and plants, provides information concerning Canada's health issues.

National Chicken Council
1015 Fifteenth Street NW, Suite 930
Washington, DC 2005-2622
(202) 296-2622
Web site: http://www.nationalchickencouncil.com
The nonprofit council represents chicken producers, processors, distributors, and related companies.

Sustainable Table
215 Lexington Avenue, Suite 1001
New York, NY 10016
(212) 991-1930
Web site: http://www.sustainabletable.org
Sustainable Table informs consumers about issues in the agricultural system. It "celebrates the possibilities and realities of the growing consumer movement toward sustainability."

POULTRY
FROM THE FARM TO YOUR TABLE

U.S. Department of Agriculture (USDA)
1400 Independence Avenue SW
Washington, DC 20250
Web site: http://www.usda.gov
The USDA publishes information on all aspects of agriculture, including food, nutrition, research, and science.

U.S. Poultry & Egg Association
1530 Cooledge Road
Tucker, GA 30084-7303
(770) 493-9401
Web site: http://www.poultryegg.org
The "world's largest poultry organization" is made up of producers and processors of broilers, turkeys, ducks, eggs, and breeding stock, as well as related companies.

Web Sites

Due to the changing nature of Internet links, Rosen Publishing has developed an online list of Web sites related to the subject of this book. This site is updated regularly. Please use this link to access the list:

http://www.rosenlinks.com/food/poult

FOR FURTHER READING

Bliss, John. *Processing Your Food* (Ethics of Food). Mankato, MN: Heinemann-Raintree, 2011.

Davis, Karen. *Prisoned Chickens Poisoned Eggs: An Inside Look at the Modern Poultry Industry*. Revised edition. Summertown, TN: Book Publishing Company, 2009.

Harmon, Daniel E. *Fish, Meat, and Poultry: Dangers in the Food Supply* (What's in Your Food? Recipe for Disaster). New York, NY: Rosen Publishing Group, 2008.

Johanson, Paula. *Fake Foods: Fried, Fast, and Processed: The Incredibly Disgusting Story* (Incredibly Disgusting Food). New York, NY: Rosen Publishing Group, 2011.

Johanson, Paula. *Processed Food* (What's in Your Food? Recipe for Disaster). New York, NY: Rosen Publishing Group, 2008.

La Bella, Laura. *Safety and the Food Supply* (In the News). New York, NY: Rosen Publishing Group, 2009.

Marjolijn, Bijlefeld, and Sharon K. Zoumbaris. *Food and You: A Guide to Healthy Habits for Teens*. Westport, CT: Greenwood Press, 2008.

Miller, Debra A. *Organic Foods* (Hot Topics). Farmington Hills, MI: Lucent, 2007.

Schlosser, Eric, and Charles Wilson. *Chew On This: Everything You Don't Want to Know About Fast Food*. Boston, MA: Houghton Mifflin, 2006.

Watson, Stephanie. *Mystery Meat: Hot Dogs, Sausages, and Lunch Meats: The Incredibly Disgusting Story* (Incredibly Disgusting Food). New York, NY: Rosen Publishing Group, 2011.

BIBLIOGRAPHY

Food, Inc. DVD. Perfect Meal, LLC, 2008.

Gogoi, Pallavi. "The Rise of the Locavore." *BusinessWeek*, May 20, 2008. Retrieved August 30, 2011 (http://www.businessweek.com/bwdaily/dnflash/content/may2008/db20080520_920283.htm).

Hegeman, Roxana. "Heat Taking Toll on U.S. Poultry Flocks." AgWeek (Associated Press), July 13, 2011. Retrieved July 2011 (http://www.agweek.com/event/article/id/18765).

"Investigation Update: Multistate Outbreak of Human Salmonella Heidelberg Infections Linked to Turkey." Centers for Disease Control and Prevention, August 18, 2011. Retrieved August 30, 2011 (http://www.cdc.gov/salmonella/heidelberg/081811/index.html).

Kirby, David. *Animal Factory*. New York, NY: St. Martin's Press, 2010.

"P. Allen Smith's Garden to Table." PBS; aired on South Carolina Educational Television, June 25, 2011 (http://www.pallensmith.com).

Pollan, Michael. *In Defense of Food: An Eater's Manifesto*. New York, NY: Penguin Press, 2008.

Pollan, Michael. *The Omnivore's Dilemma: The Secrets Behind What You Eat*. New York, NY: Dial Books, 2009.

Schlosser, Eric. *Fast Food Nation: The Dark Side of the All-American Meal*. Boston, MA: Houghton Mifflin, 2001.

Winne, Mark. *Food Rebels, Guerrilla Gardeners, and Smart-Cookin' Mamas: Fighting Back in an Age of Industrial Agriculture*. Boston, MA: Beacon Press, 2010.

INDEX

A
additives, 20, 21, 24, 26, 31
American Poultry Association, 10

C
CAFOs, 17
Canadian Food Inspection Agency, 34
Centers for Disease Control and Prevention (CDC), 5, 32
Chew On This, 18–19, 22, 31, 34

E
eggs, 8, 9, 10, 11, 13, 21, 25, 26–27, 28, 29, 32, 33, 34, 36

F
farmers' markets, 13, 40
food labels, 17, 20, 22, 26, 40
FoodNet, 34
Food Safety and Inspection Service (FSIS), 24, 26
free-range birds, 20–21, 36, 40

G
game birds, 10–11, 17, 36
genetic engineering, 18

I
In Defense of Food, 30, 40
irradiation, 31

L
Listeria, 5–6, 31–32, 36
locavore movement, 39–41

N
National Chicken Council, 6, 8, 34
National Turkey Federation, 13, 34
nutritionist, questions to ask a, 36

O
Omnivore's Dilemma, The, 12, 20, 39
organic products, 20, 21, 37–38, 39

P
People for the Ethical Treatment of Animals (PETA), 38
Pollan, Michael, 12, 20, 21, 30, 39, 40
poultry
  farming, raising, 13–14, 15–21, 37–41
  health/safety issues, 29–35
  myths/facts, 28
  overview, 4–14
  processing/packaging, 22–27
Poultry Products Inspection Act, 34

S
salmonellosis, 4, 5, 6, 24, 28
Schlosser, Eric, 18, 22, 23, 31, 34

U
U.S. Department of Agriculture (USDA), 20, 24, 33–34, 35
U.S. Food and Drug Administration (FDA), 26, 34

V
vegans, 29

W
Wilson, Charles, 18, 22, 23, 31, 34

POULTRY
FROM THE FARM TO YOUR TABLE

About the Author

Daniel E. Harmon is a veteran magazine and newspaper editor and writer whose articles have appeared in many national and regional periodicals. He has written numerous books for young adults, covering topics such as obesity; fish, meat, and poultry; the Food and Drug Administration; and the Environmental Protection Agency. He lives in Spartanburg, South Carolina.

Photo Credits

Cover, p. 1 (rooster, chicken) © www.istockphoto.com/Liliya Drifan; cover, pp. 1, 3, 7, 15, 22, 29, 37 (packaged chicken) © www.istockphoto.com/onebluelight; cover, pp. 1, 28 (towel) © www.istockphoto.com/milanfoto; p. 3 (packaged chicken) © www.istockphoto.com/Floortje, (packaged turkey) © www.istockphoto.com/Debbi Smirnoff; pp. 4–5 Kevin Dietsch/UPI/Landov; p. 7 (bottom) Ciaran Griffin/Stockbyte/Thinkstock; p. 9 © www.istockphoto.com/Barbara Gibbons; p. 11 GraÃ§a Victoria/Shutterstock.com; p. 13 www.istockphoto.com/Thinkstock; pp. 16, 27 © AP Images; p. 19 Joern Pollex/Getty Images; pp. 21, 26 Shutterstock.com; p. 23 Glowimages/Getty Images; p. 30 David Silverman/Getty Images; p. 32 © Science Faction/SuperStock; p. 33 Sally Ullman/FoodPix/Getty Images; p. 35 Photo by Keith Weller, USDA Agriculture Research Service; p. 36 (figure) © www.istockphoto.com/Max Delson Martins Santos, (measuring tape) © www.istockphoto.com/Zoran Kolundzija; p. 38 John Lee/Aurora/Getty Images; p. 41 Baerbel Schmidt/Stone/Getty Image.

Designer: Nelson Sá; Editor: Kathy Kuhtz Campbell;
Photo Researcher: Karen Huang